The
Wonderful
World of
Flowers
Coloring Book

The Wonderful World of Flowers

Coloring Book

Let your imagination blossom

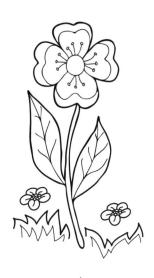

SIRIUS

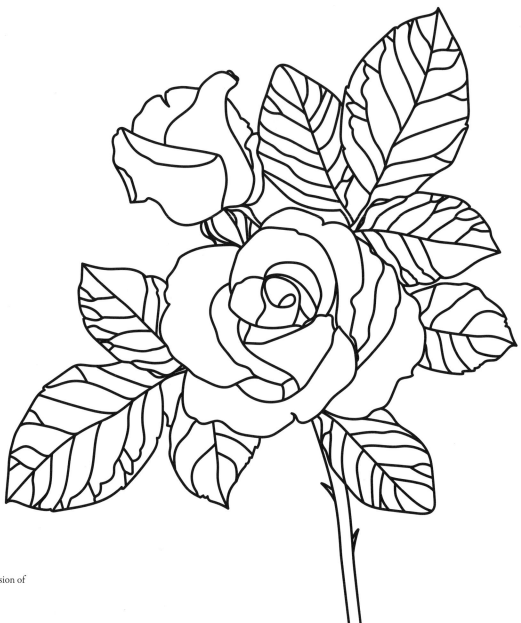

SIRIUS

This edition published in 2024 by Sirius Publishing, a division of
Arcturus Publishing Limited,
26/27 Bickels Yard, 151–153 Bermondsey Street,
London SE1 3HA

ISBN: 978-1-3988-3664-8
CH011161NT
Supplier 29, Date 1123, PI 00005348

Printed in China

Introduction

Color your way into a glorious world of flowers. It doesn't matter if you're not a keen gardener or flower arranger—you can have a true artist's appreciation for flowers. They are a favorite theme for art and decoration, with their delicate shapes and exquisite colors, and a great subject for coloring in as well. Collected here are naturally rendered blooms including lilies, roses, dahlias, chrysanthemums, and irises. Others appear as sumptuous bouquets or arranged in vases, jugs, or even an appealing wooden bucket. Some are worked into specially designed mandalas with flowers at their heart, while elsewhere there is an array of patterns, some elaborate and classical, others more modernistic and graphic in styling. The flowers here allow you to use your imagination and skill at putting together colors. You don't have to follow a natural palette—you can choose your hues according to your mood. Find a quiet place in your home, or perhaps in a garden or park, along with a selection of pencils, pens, or markers, and take the time you need to create a joyous floral artwork.

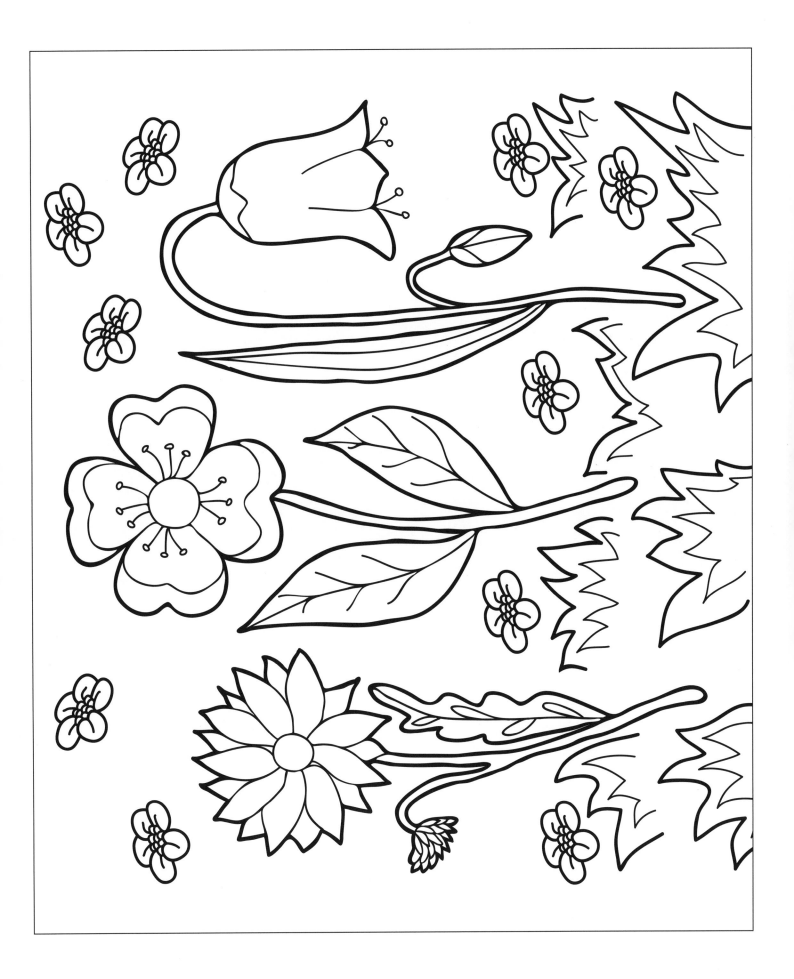

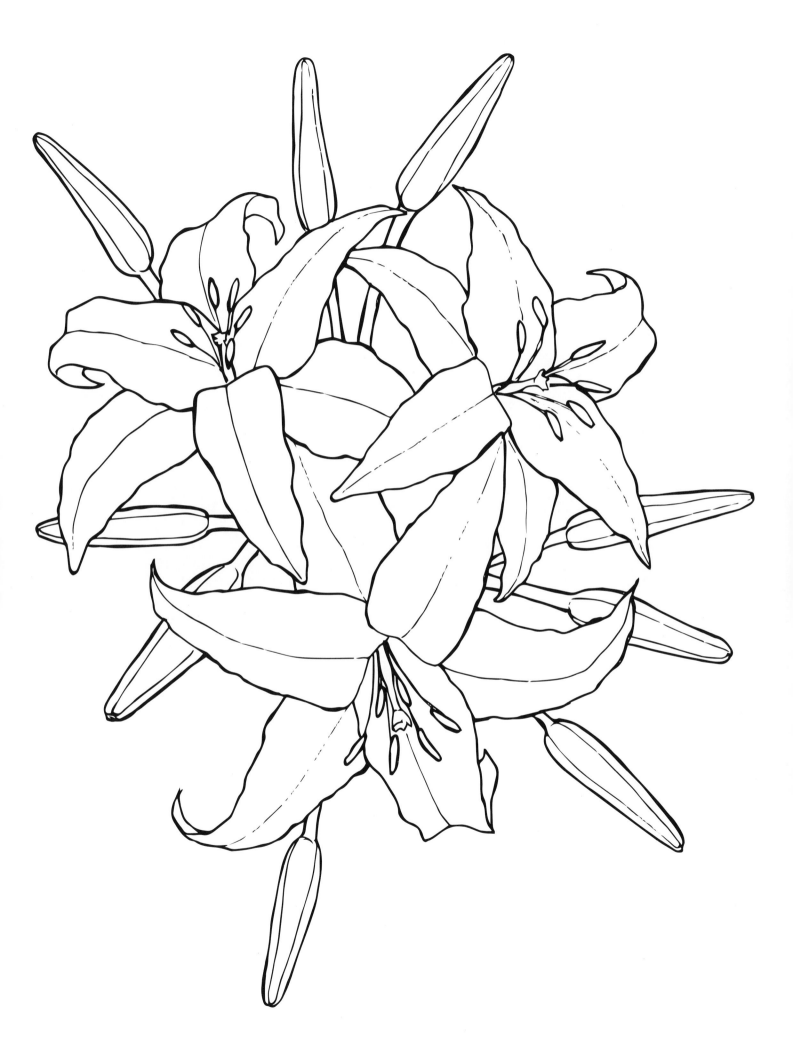

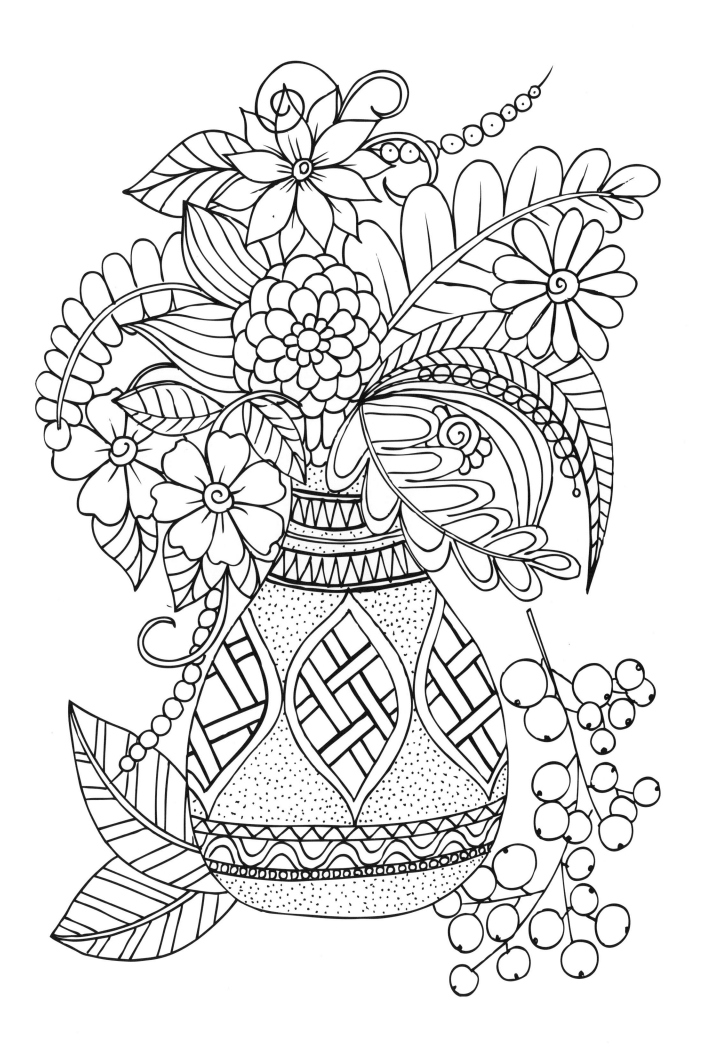

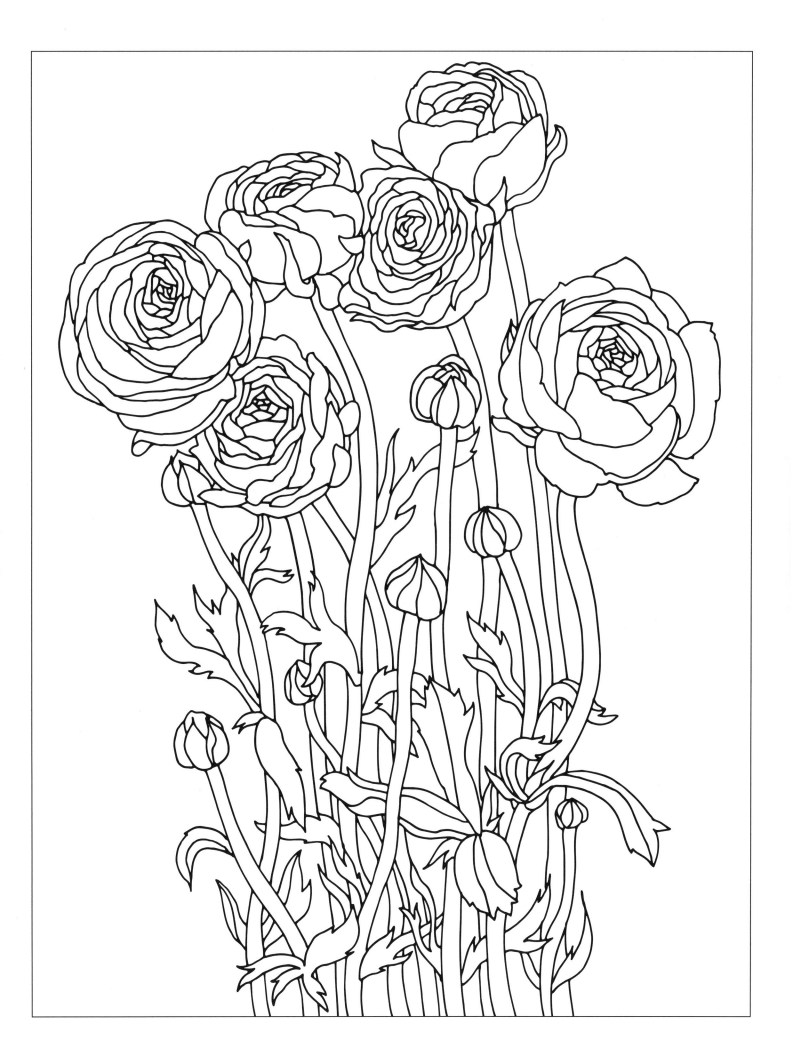

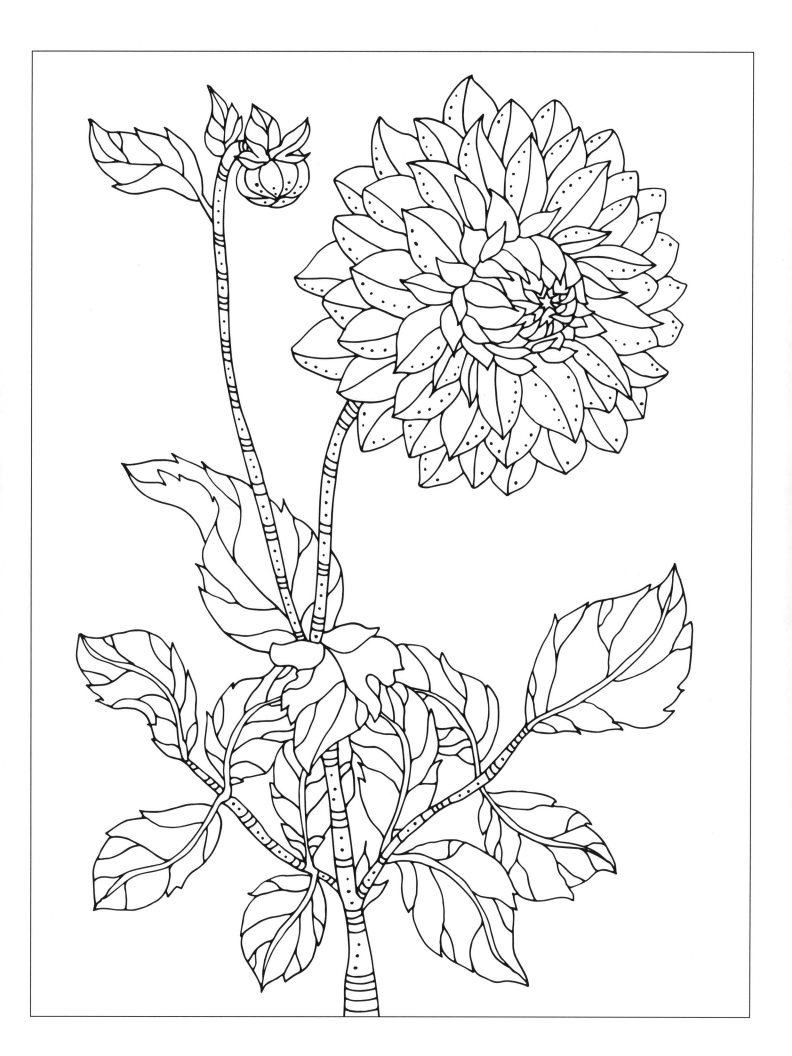

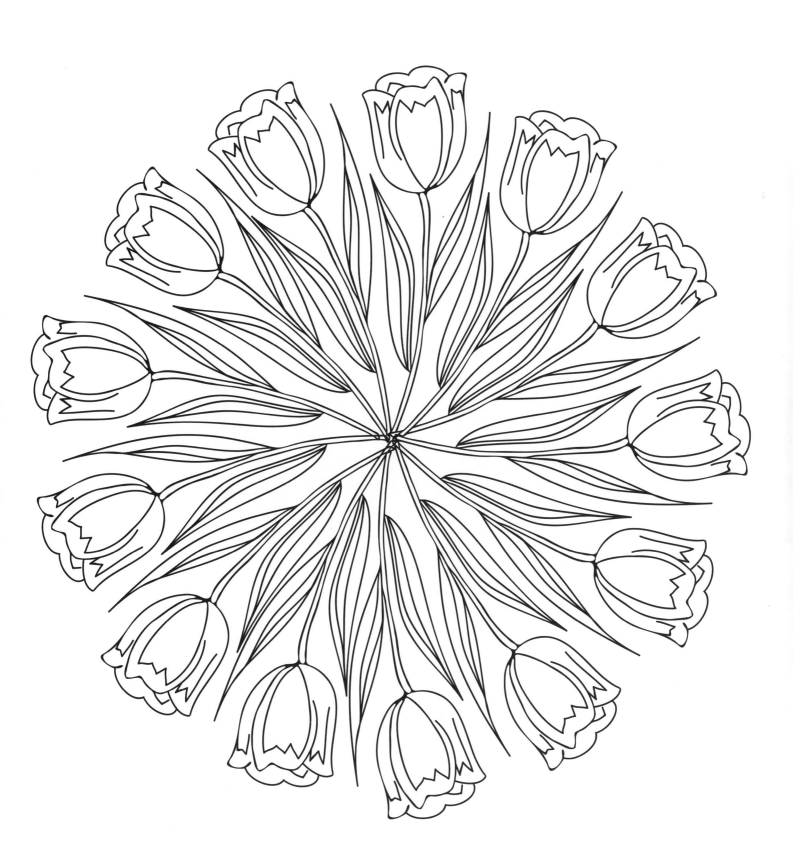

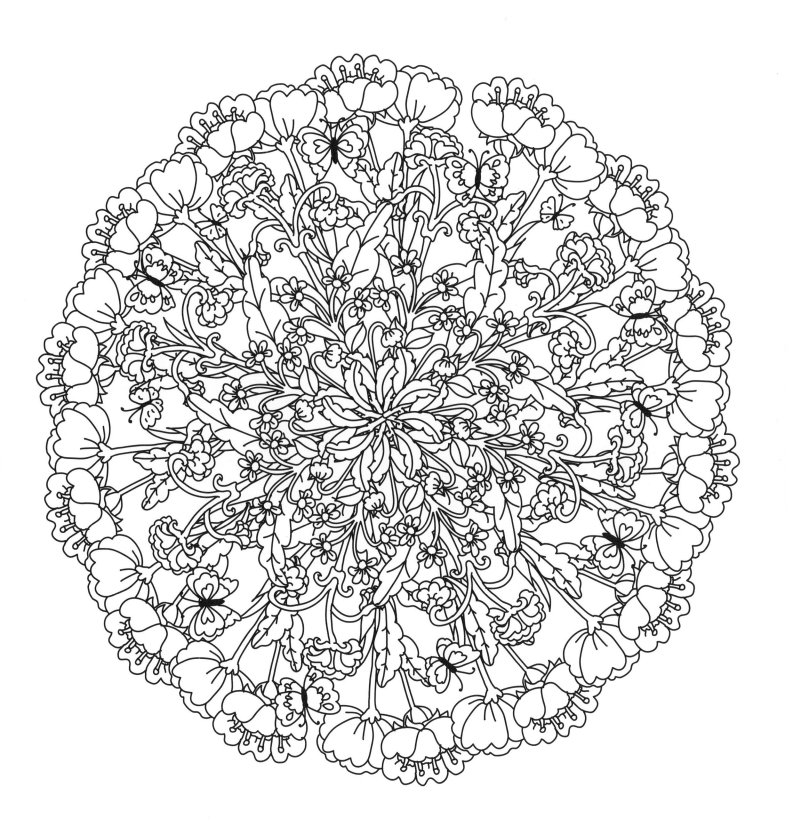

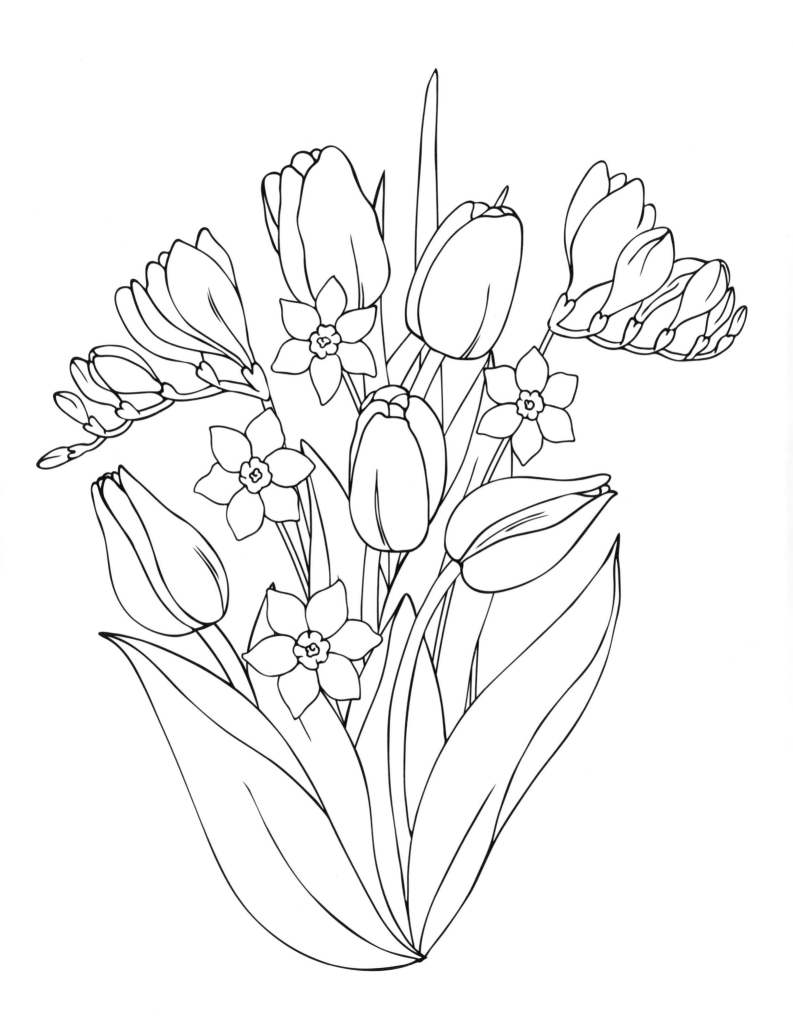

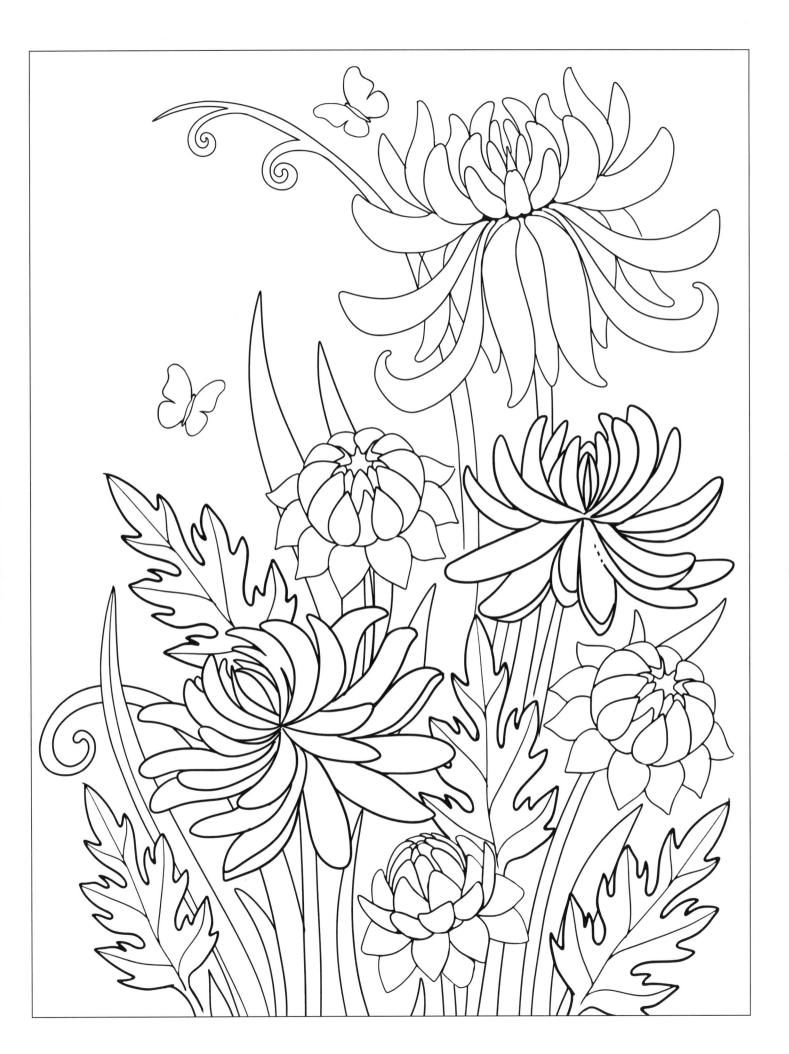

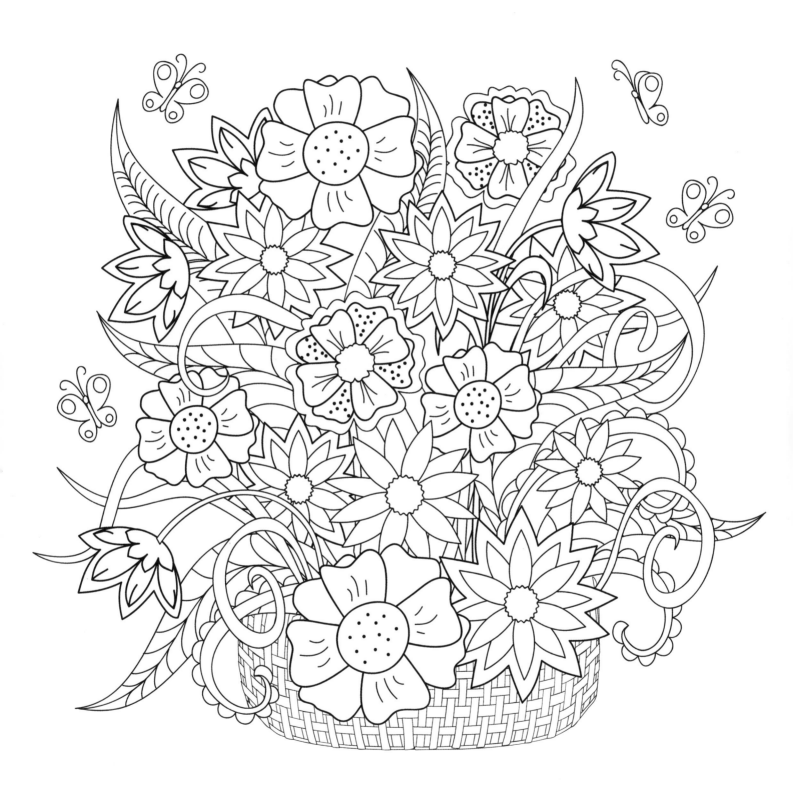

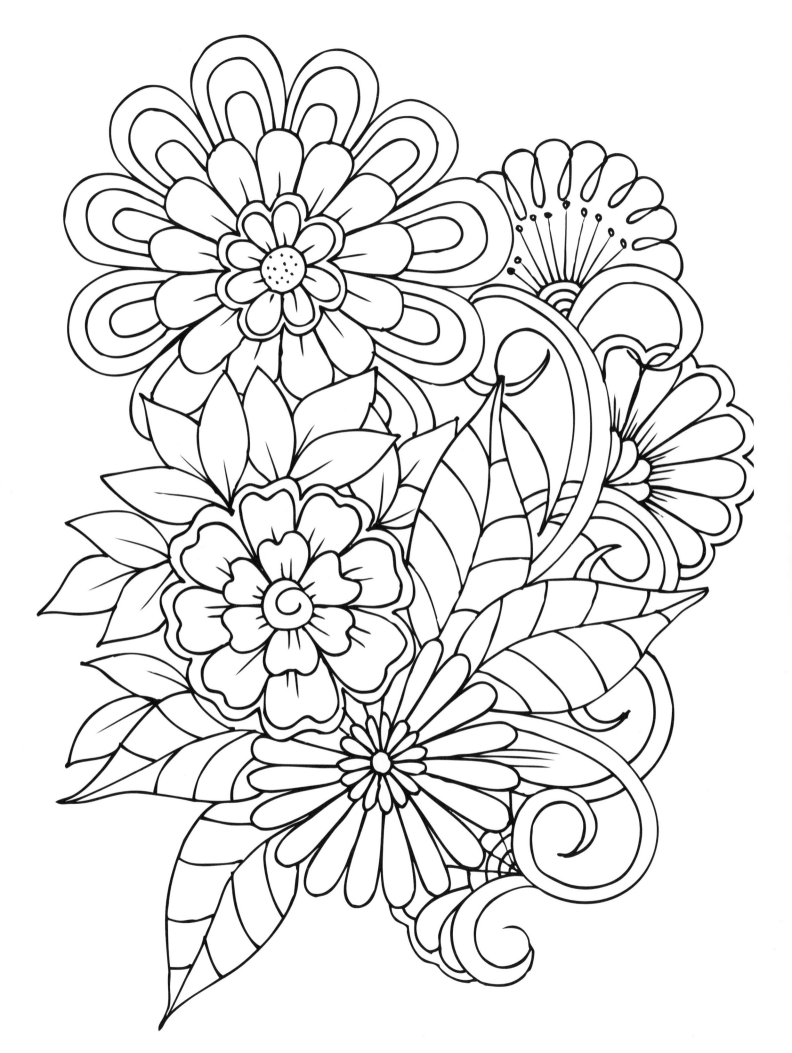

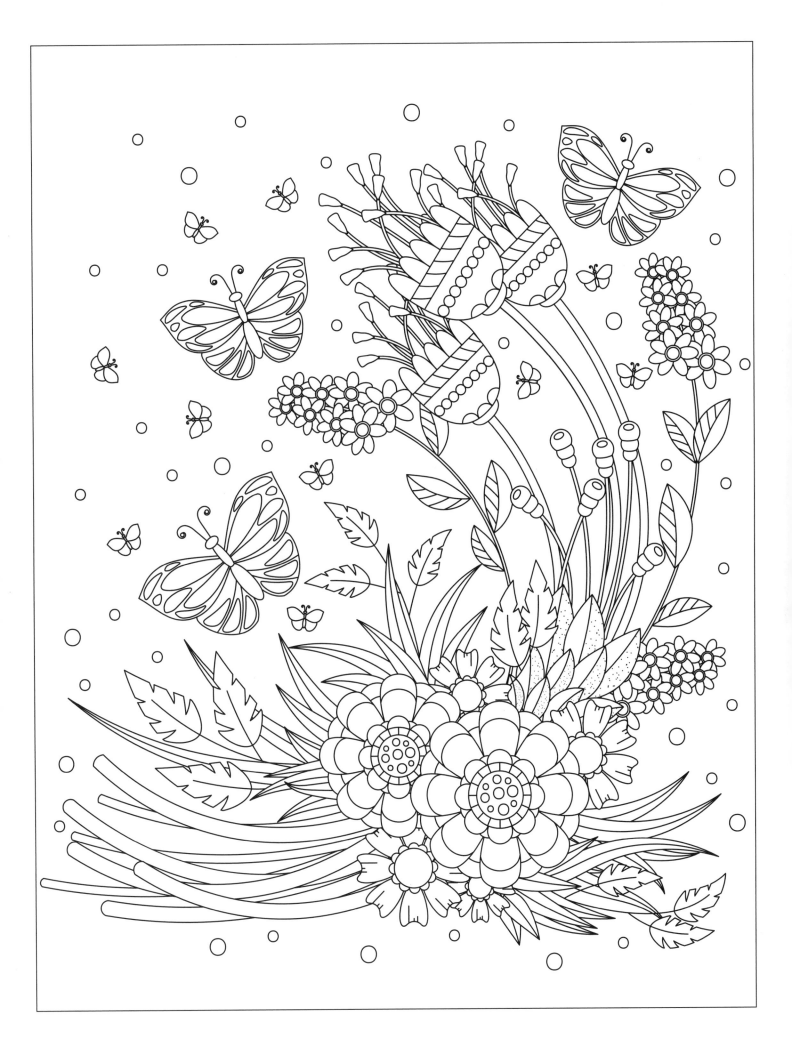

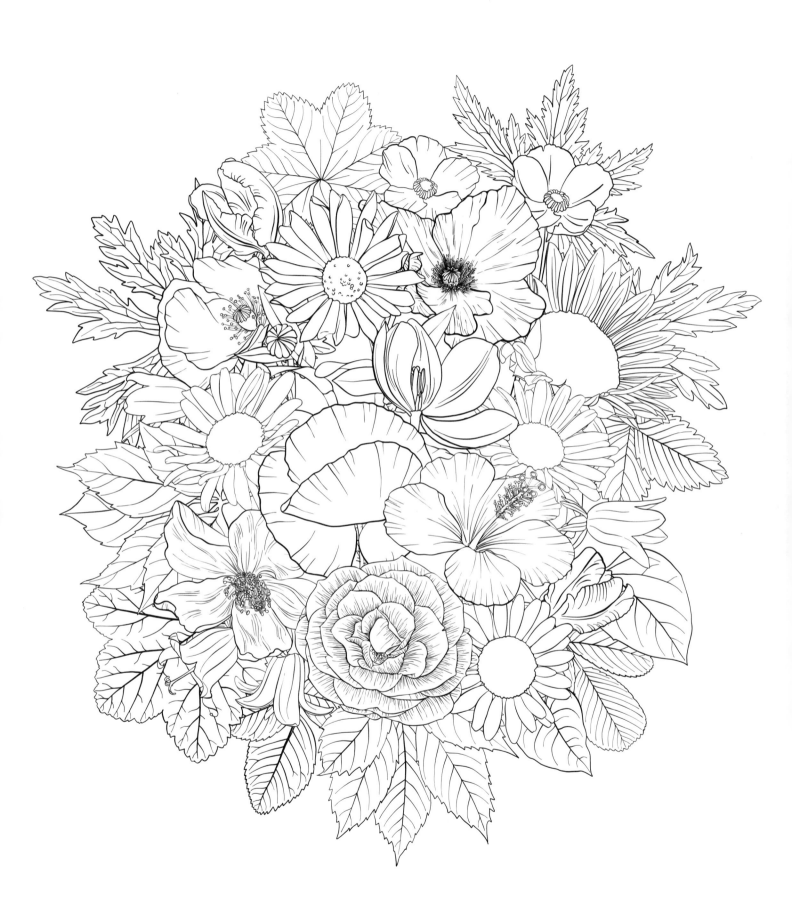

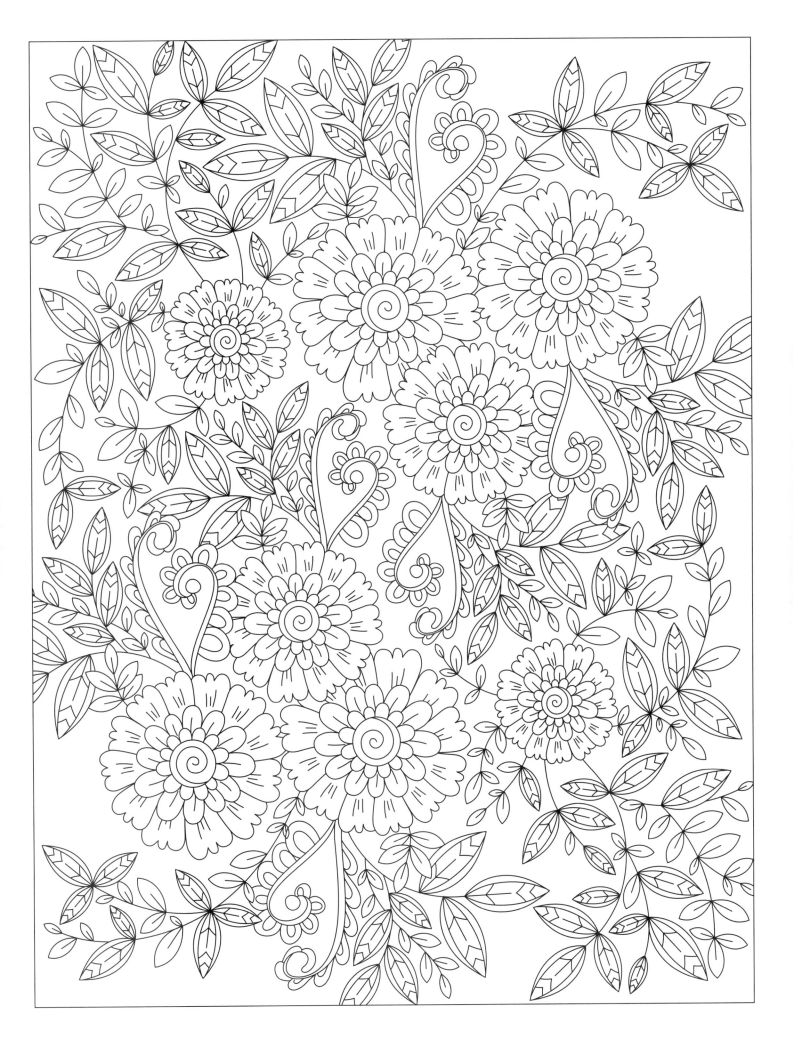

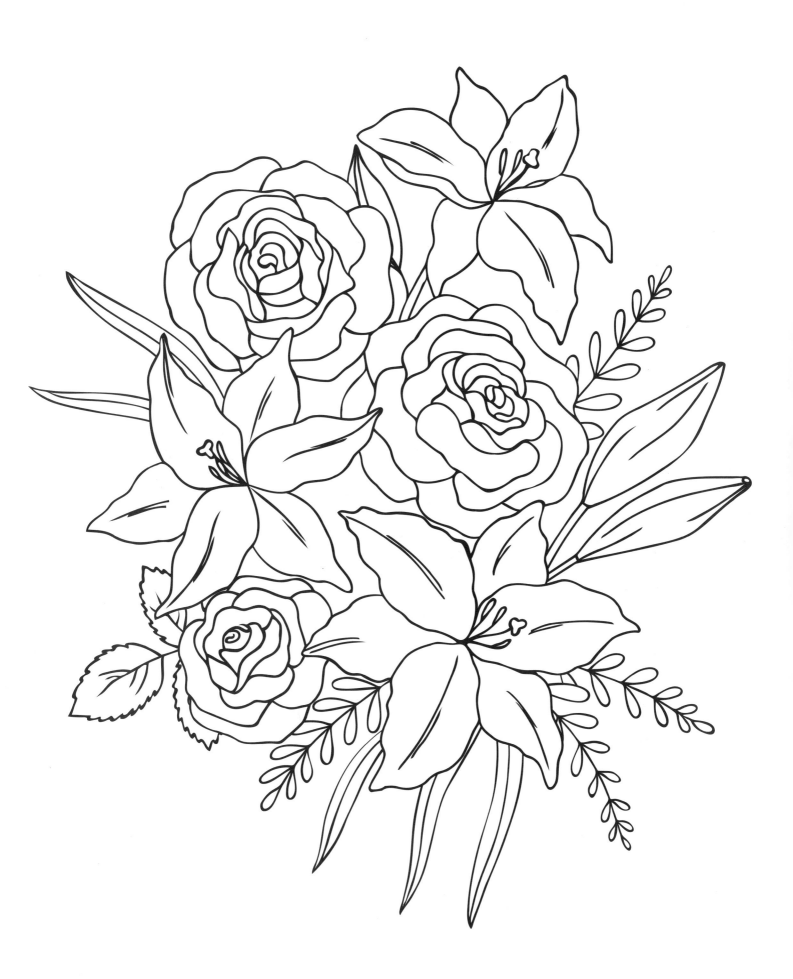

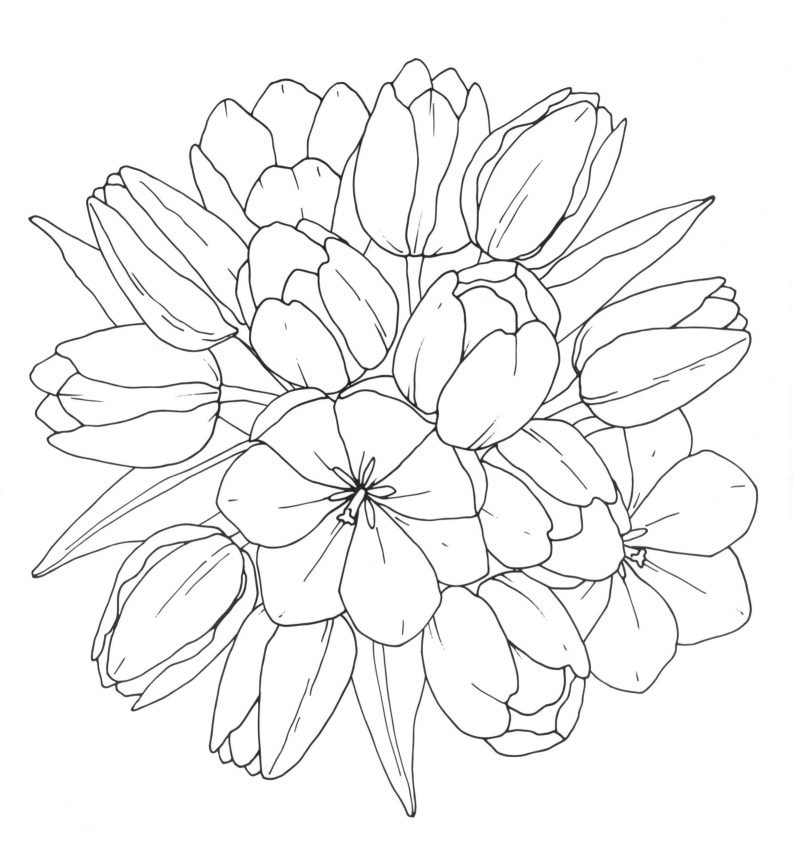

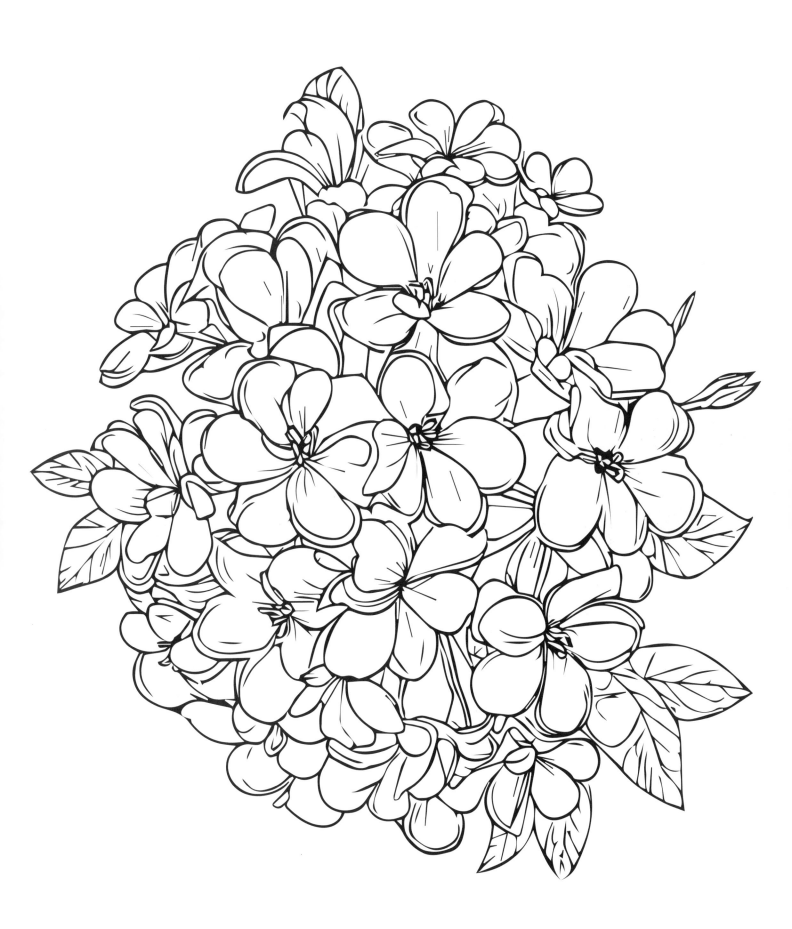

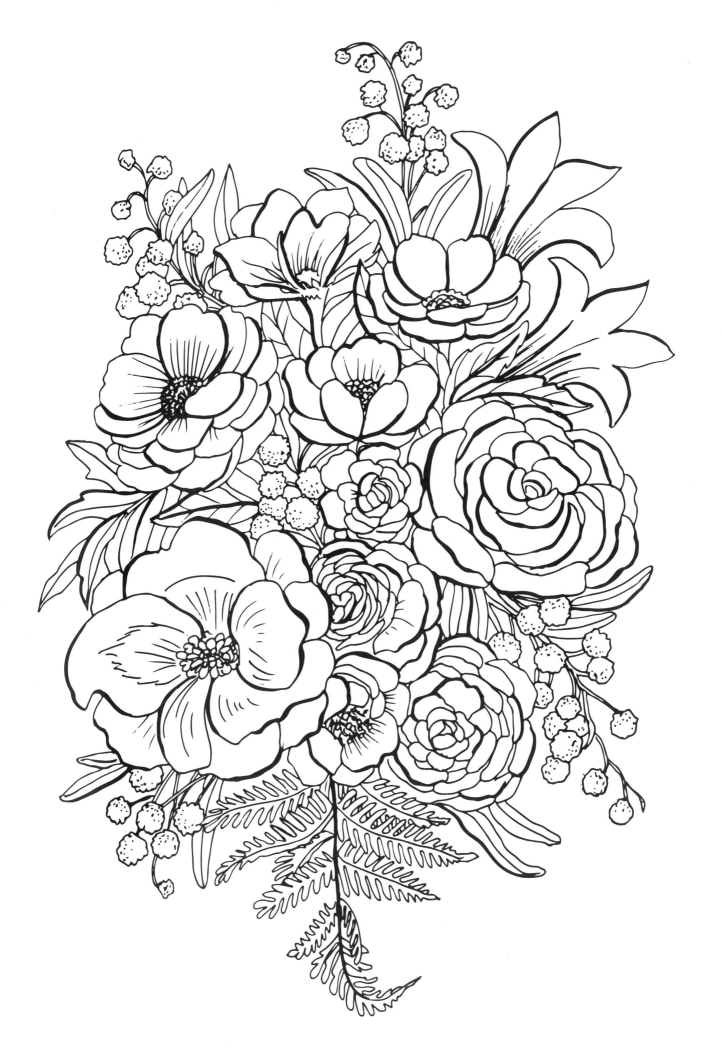

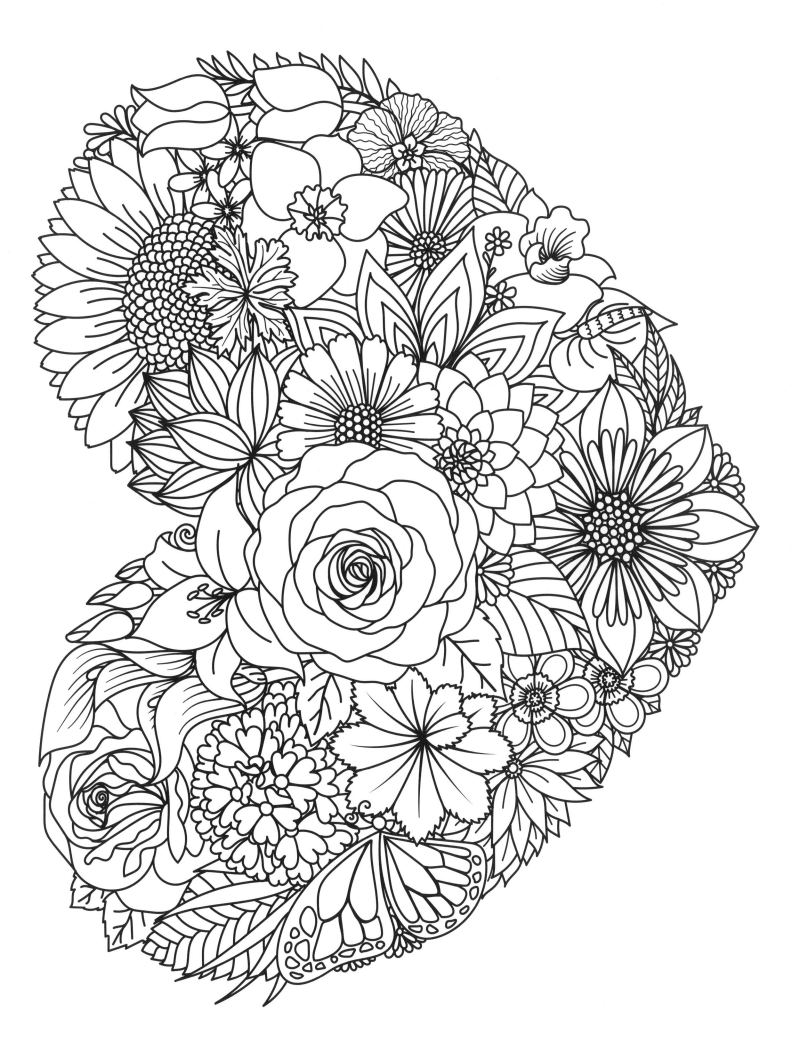

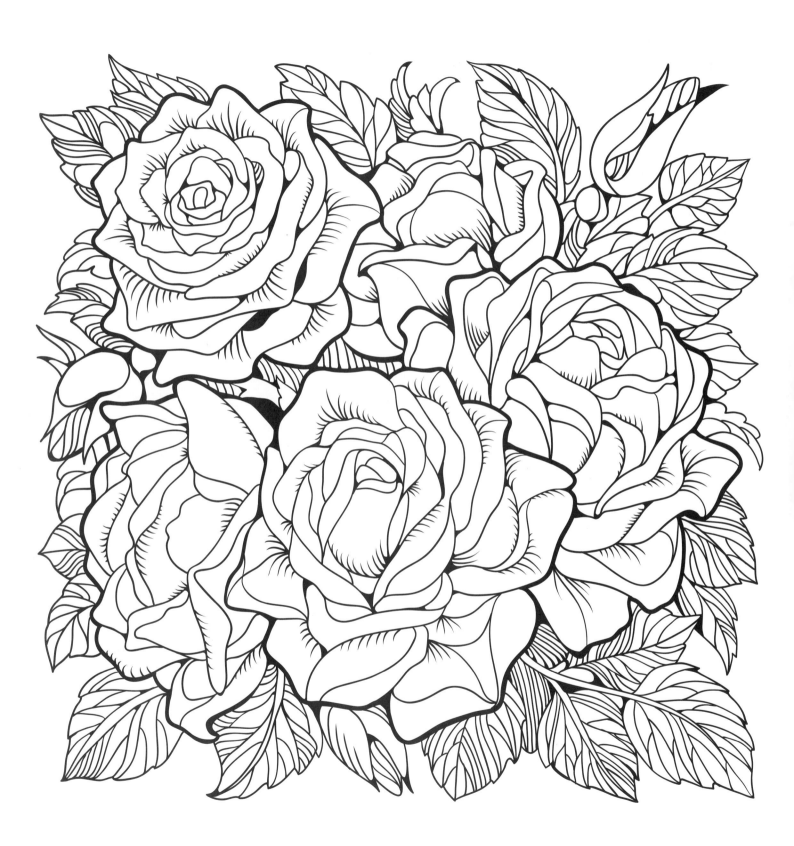

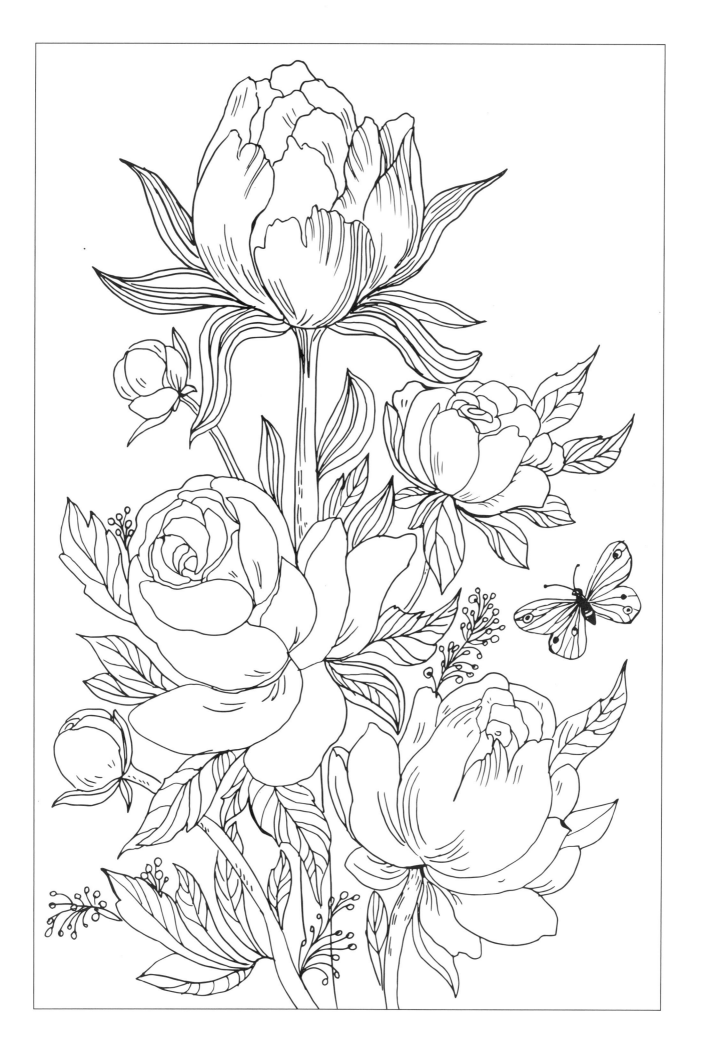

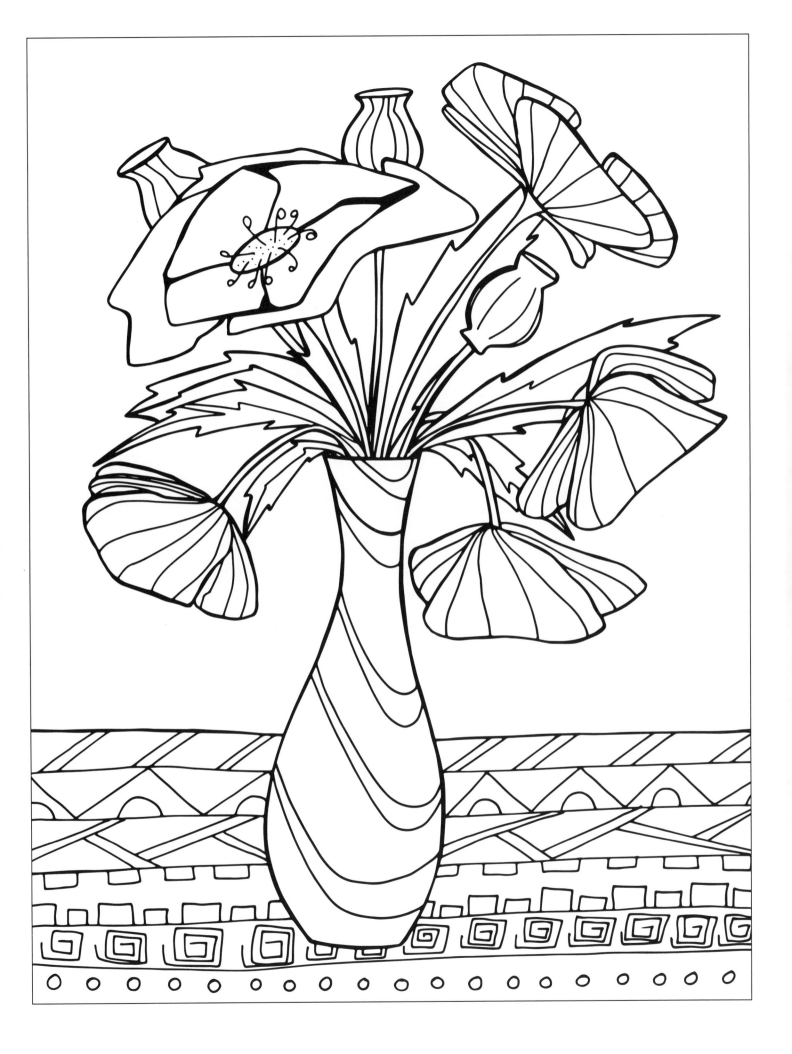

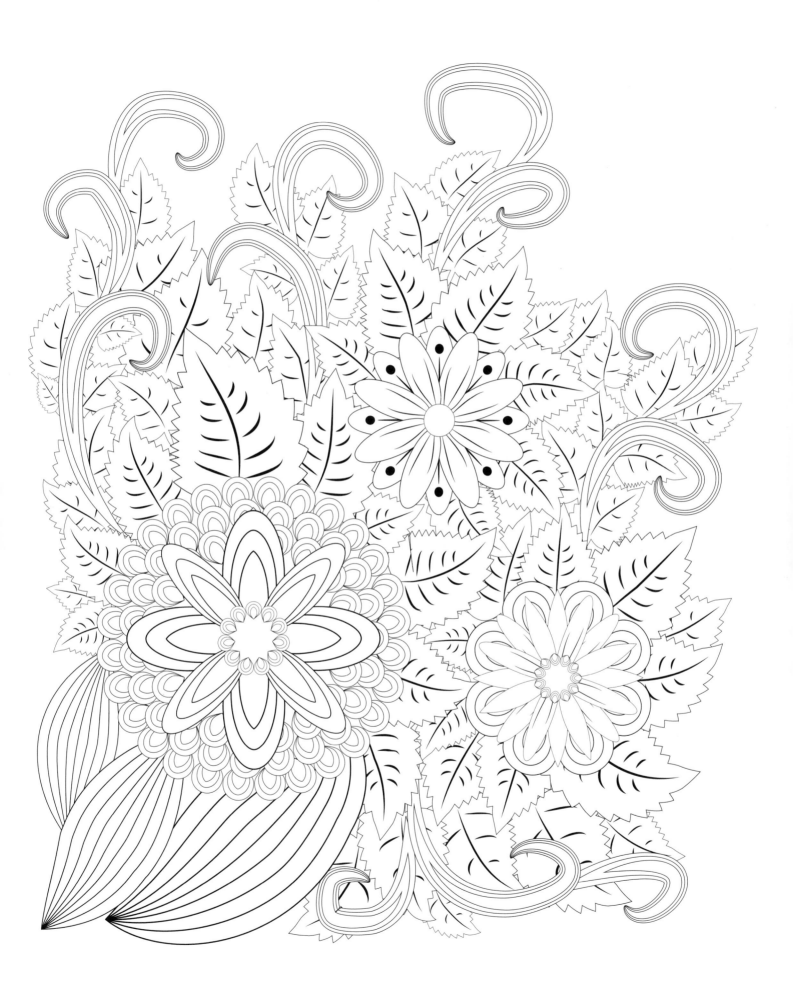

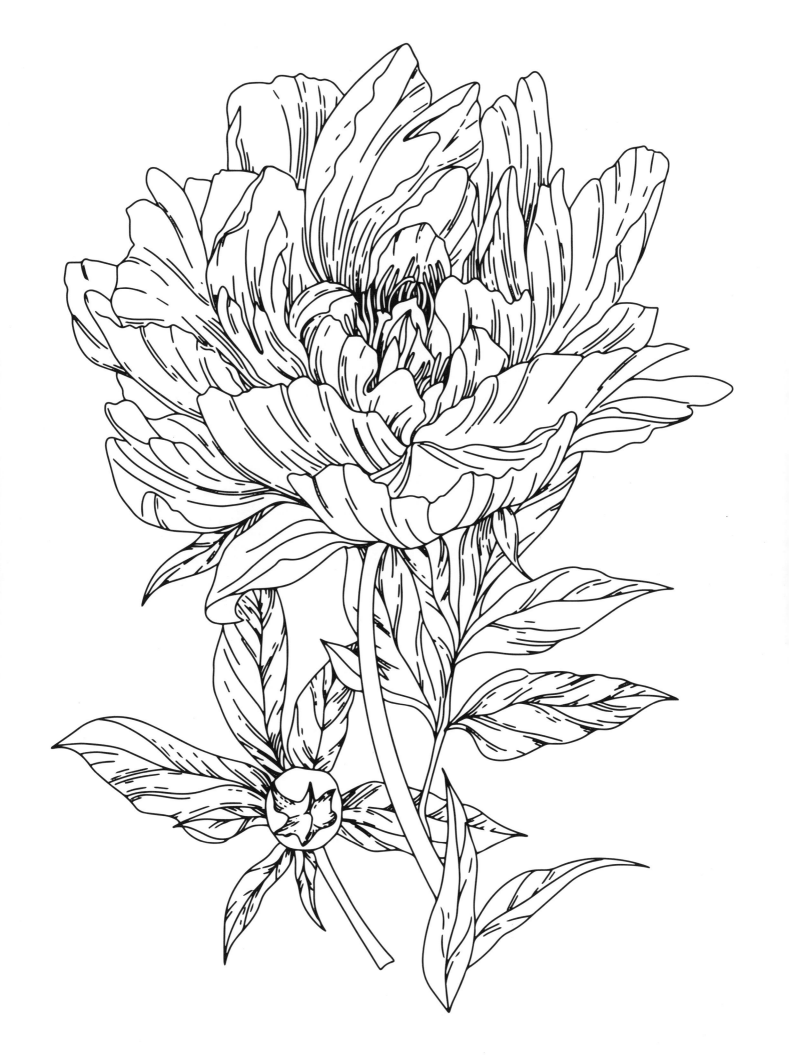

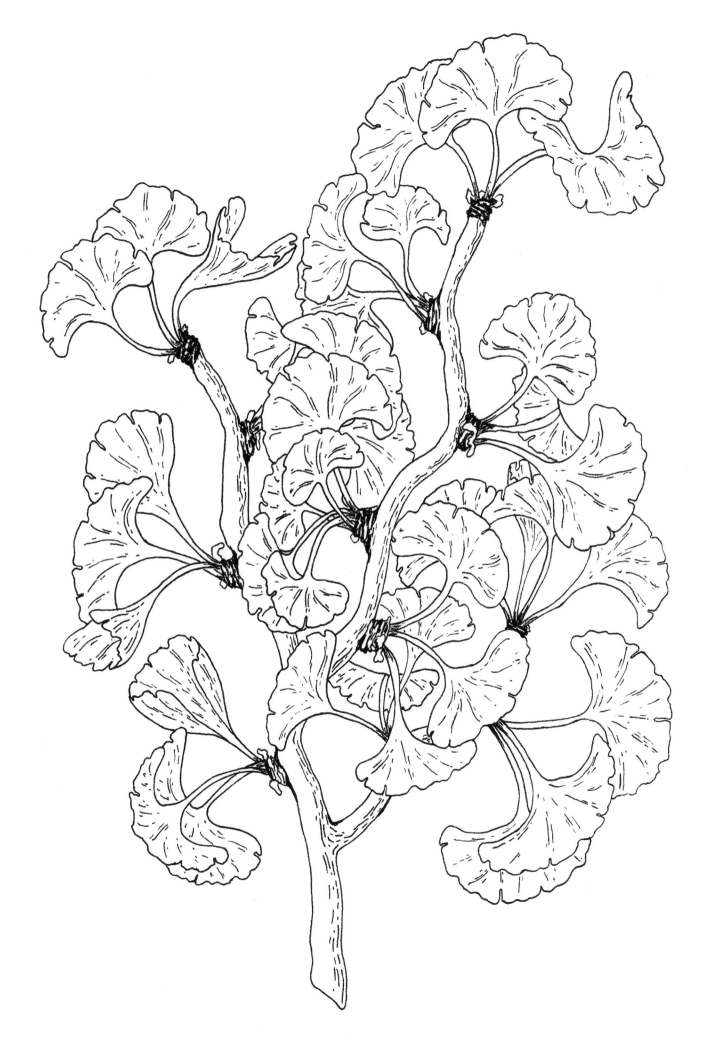

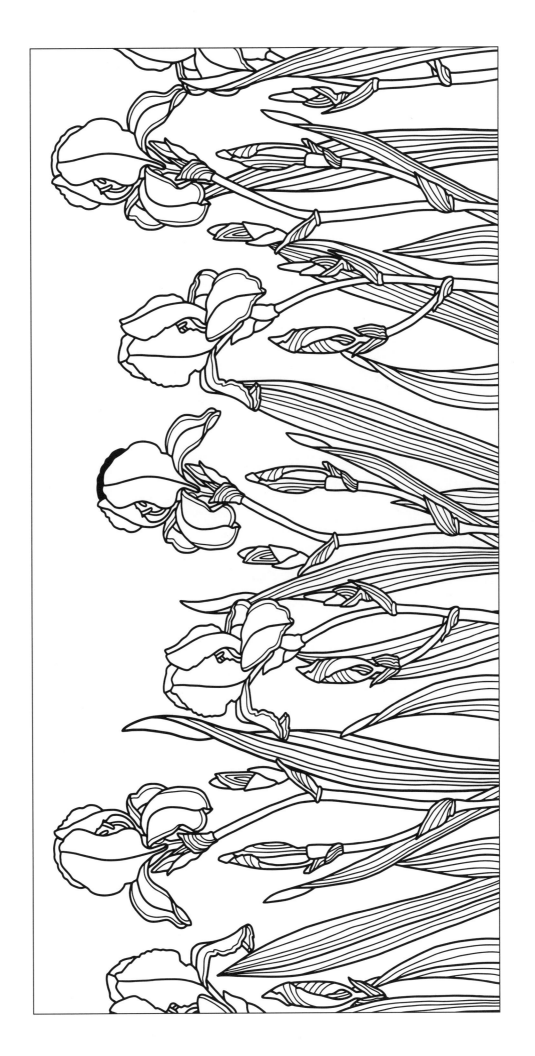

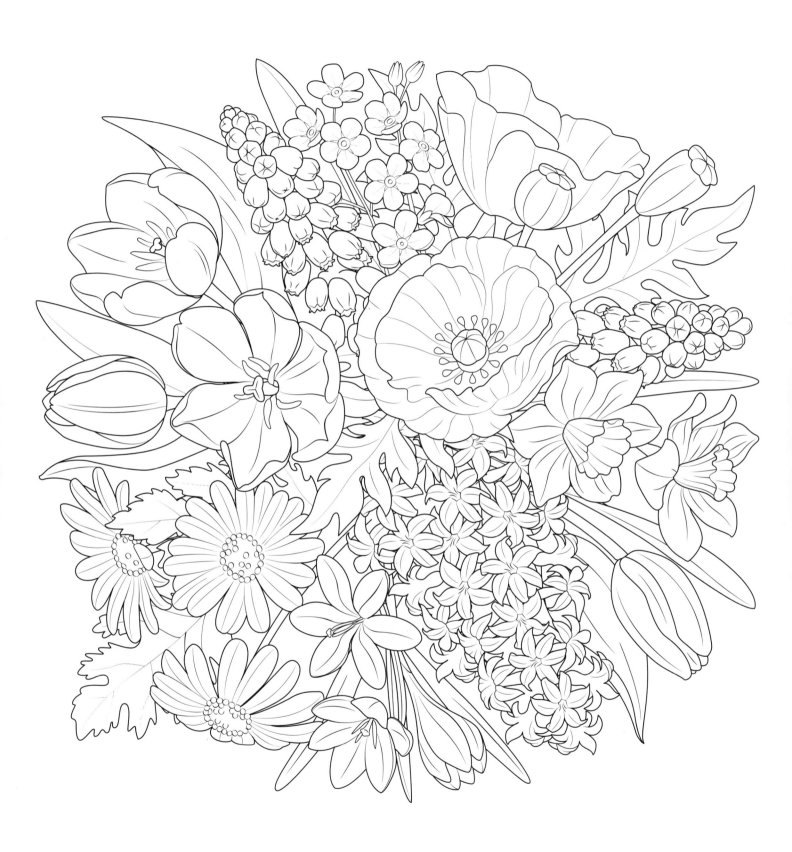

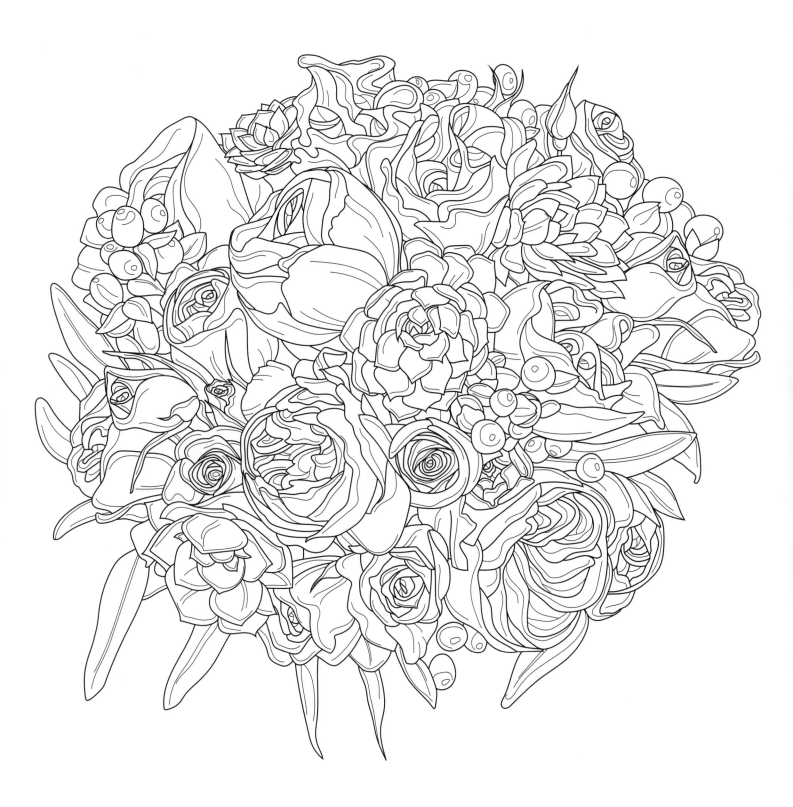

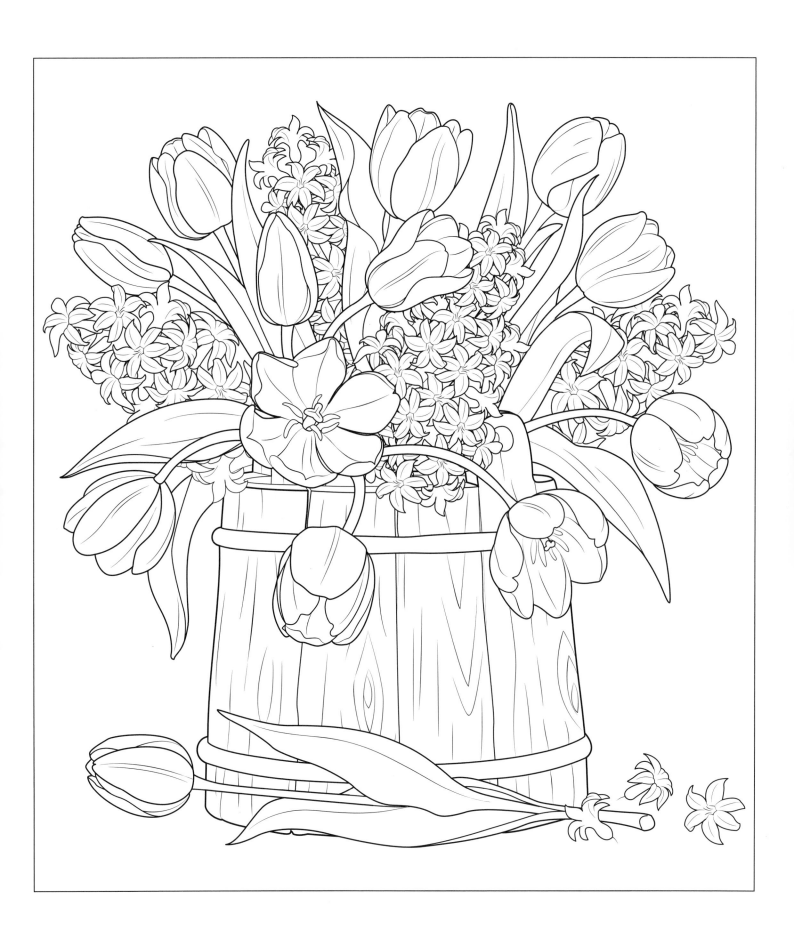

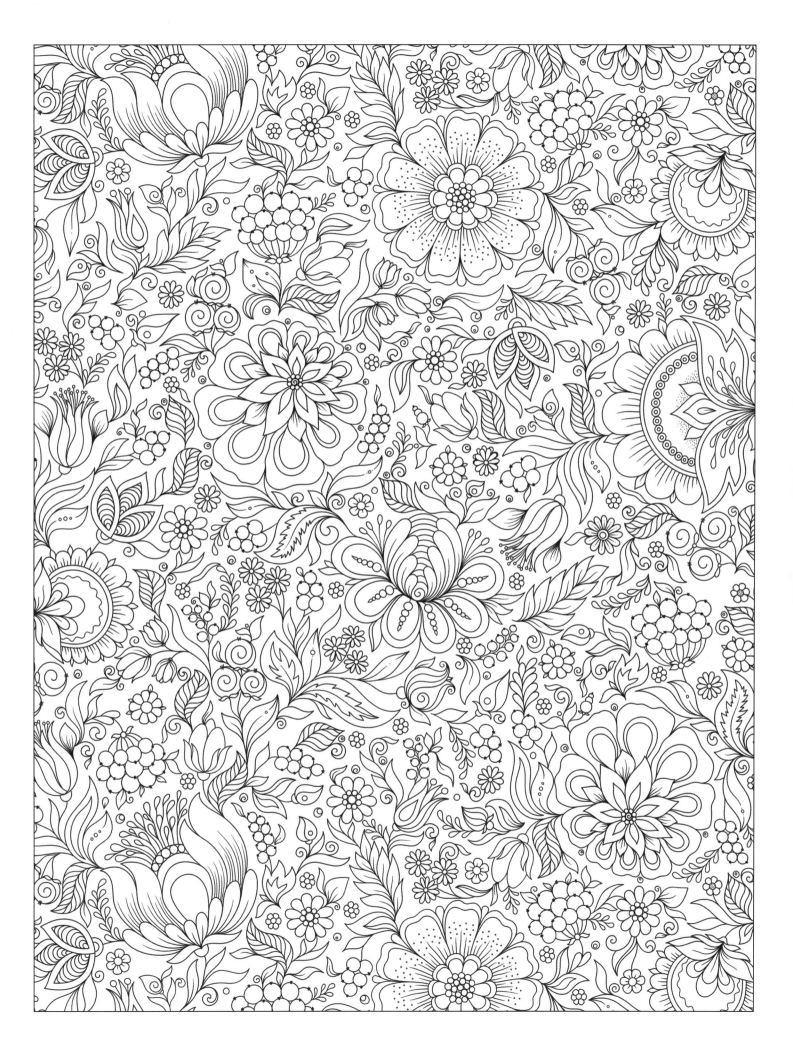

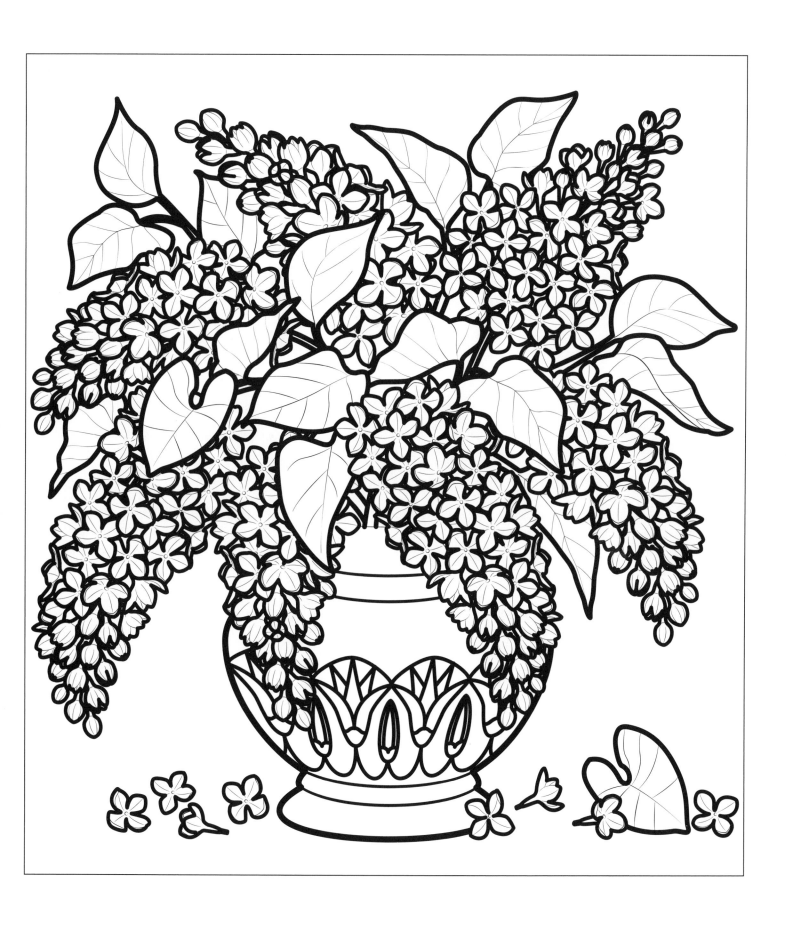

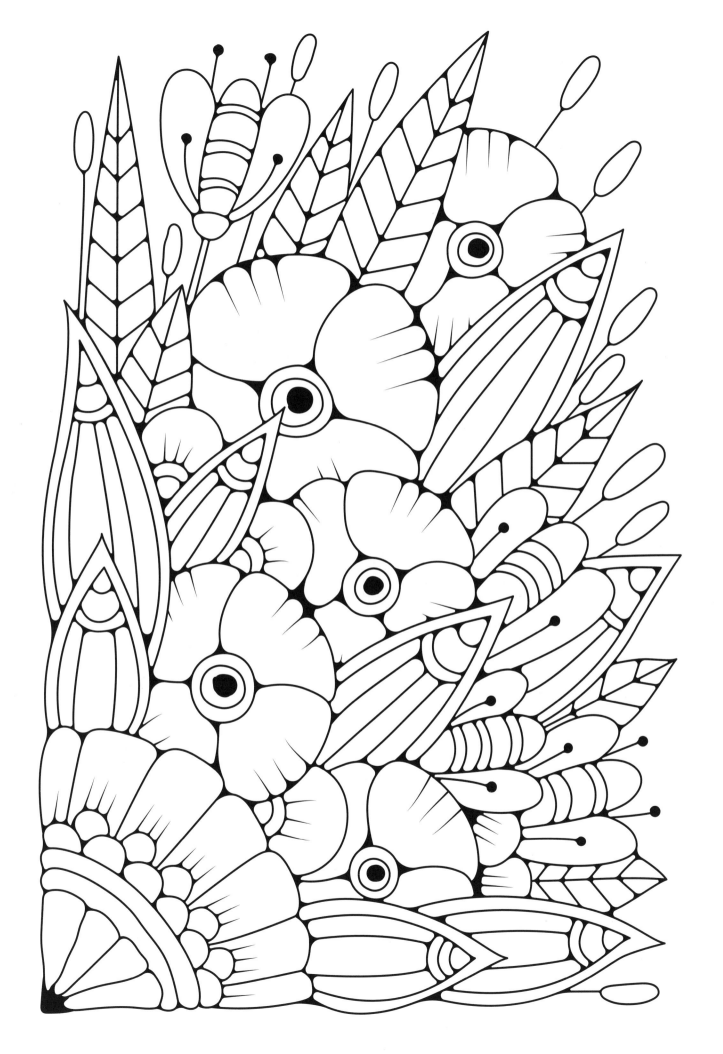

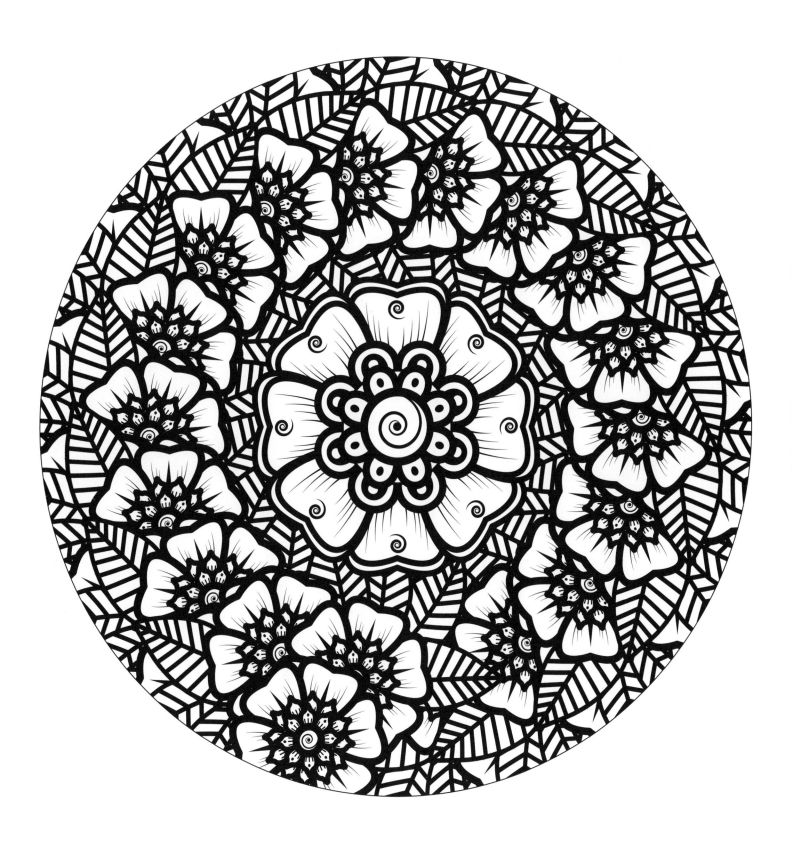

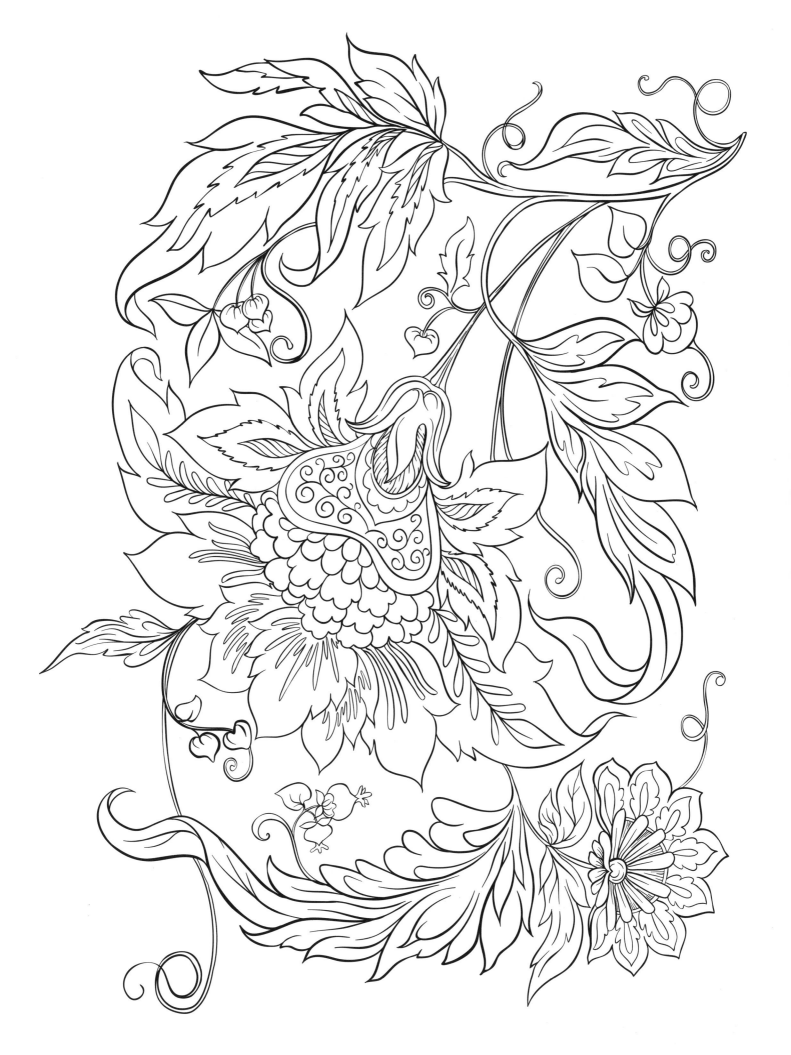

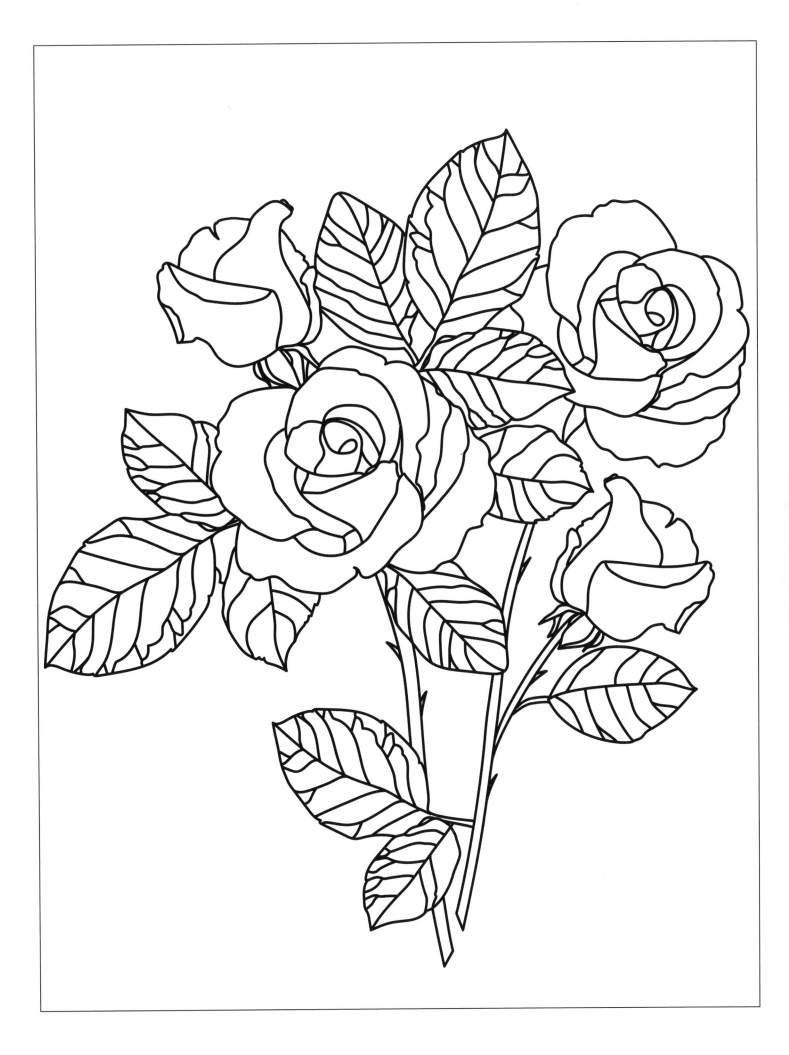

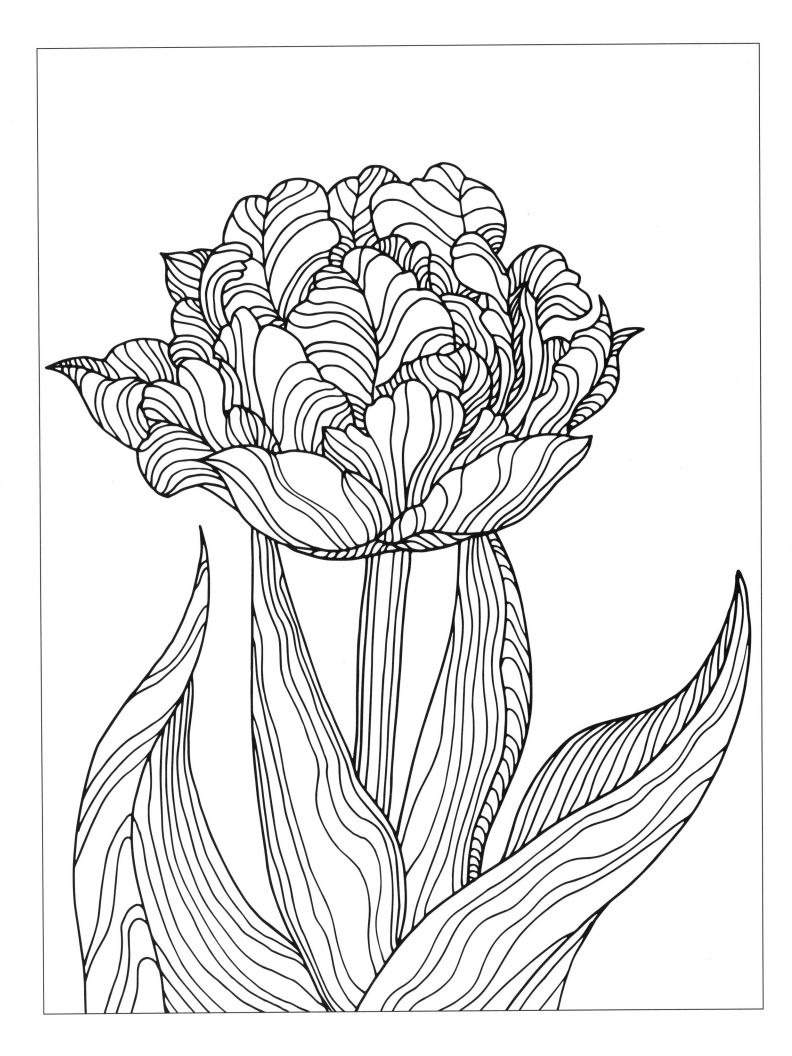

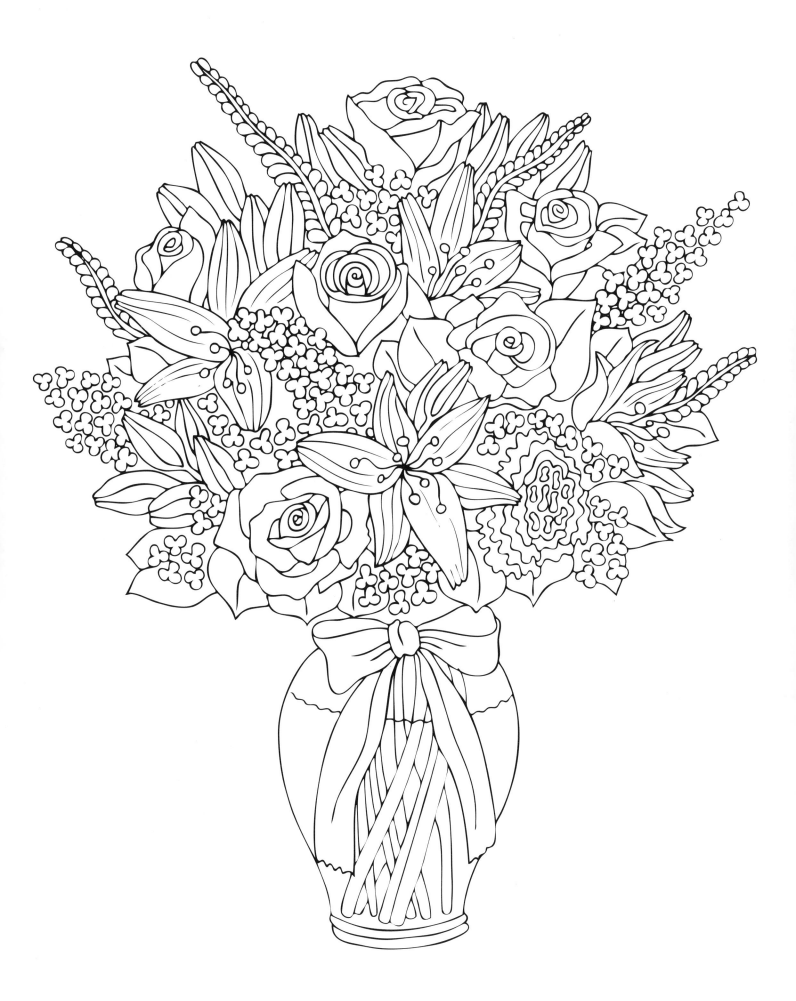

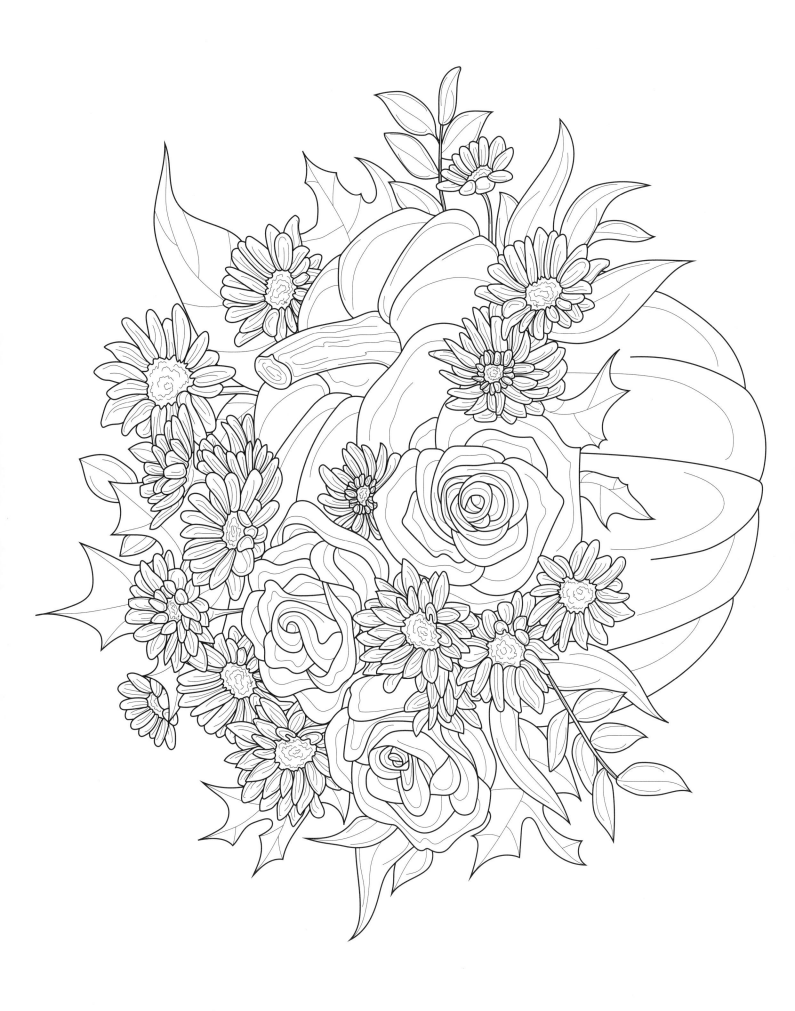

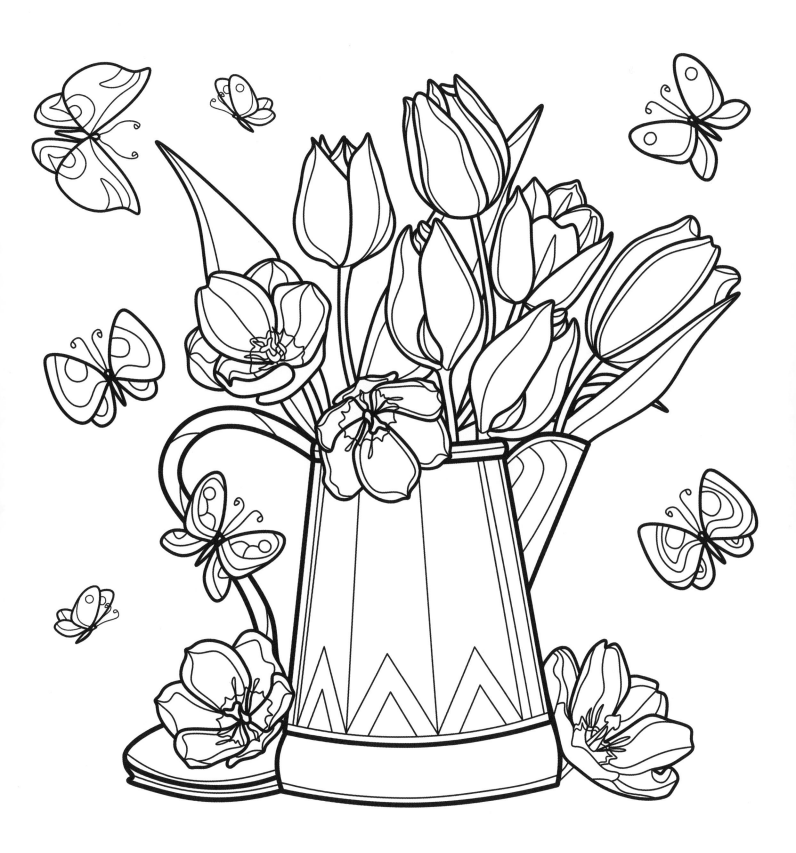

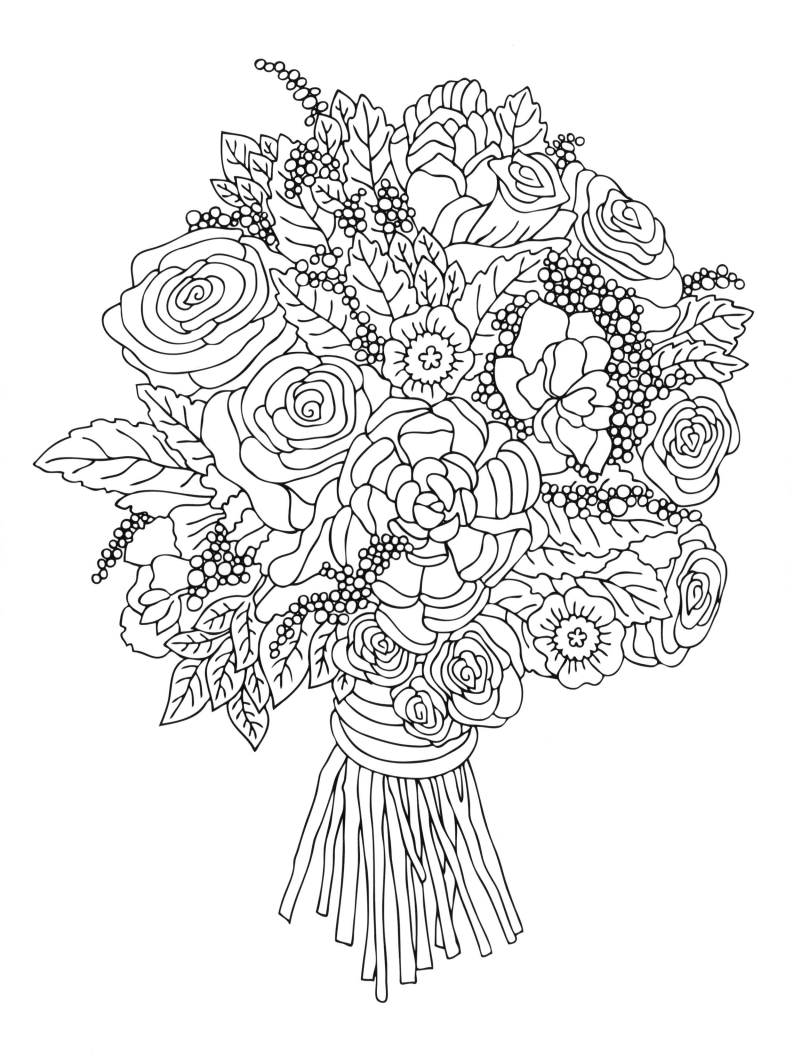

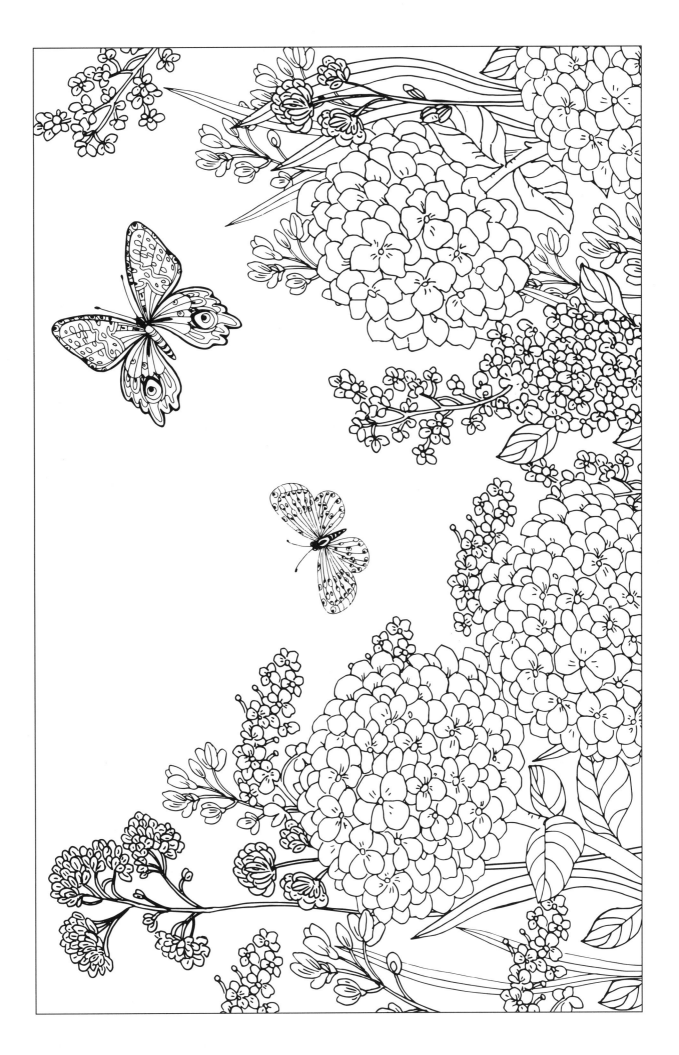

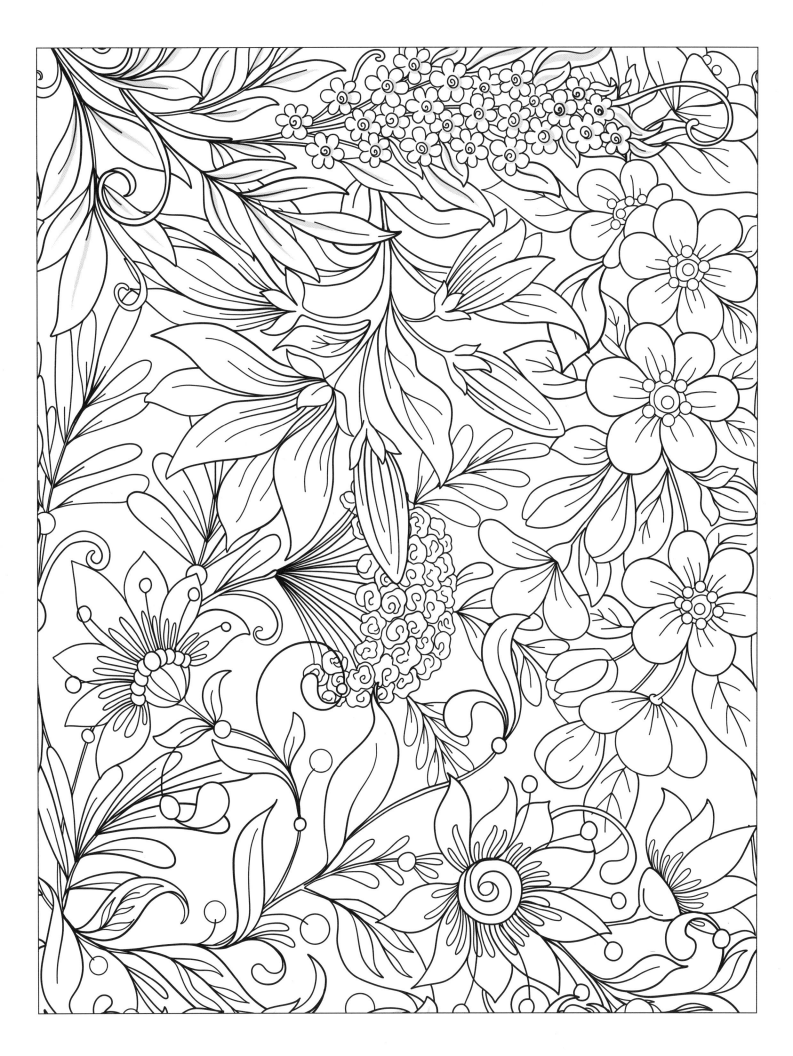

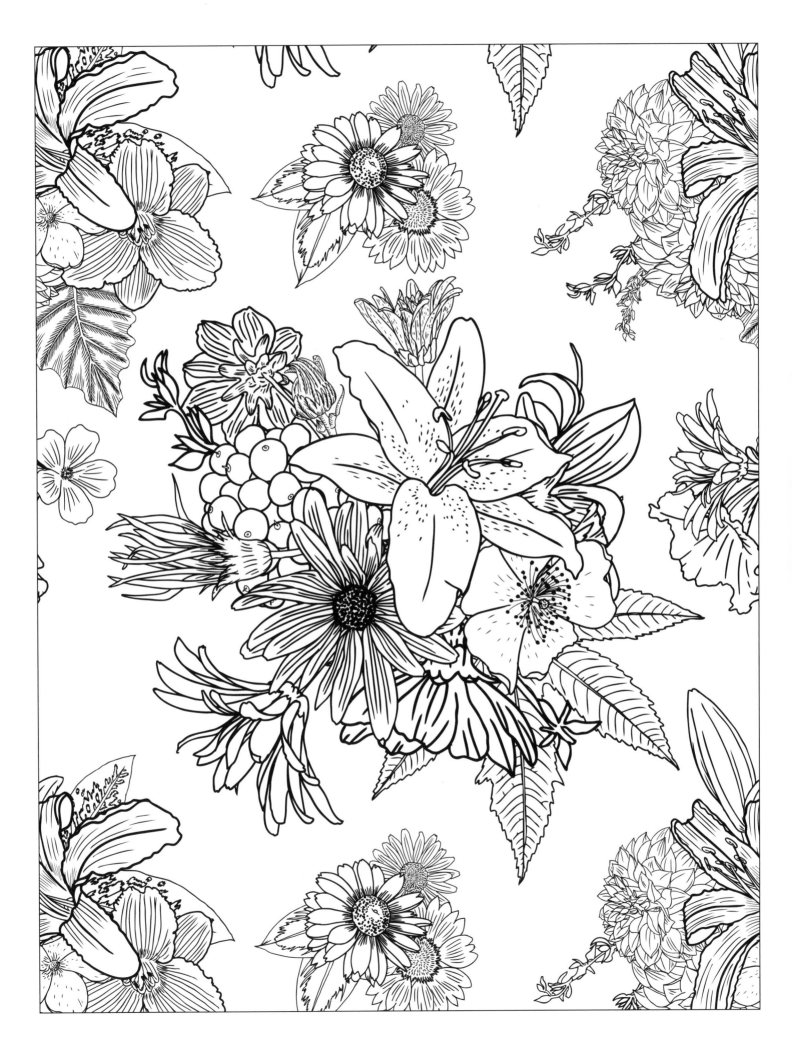

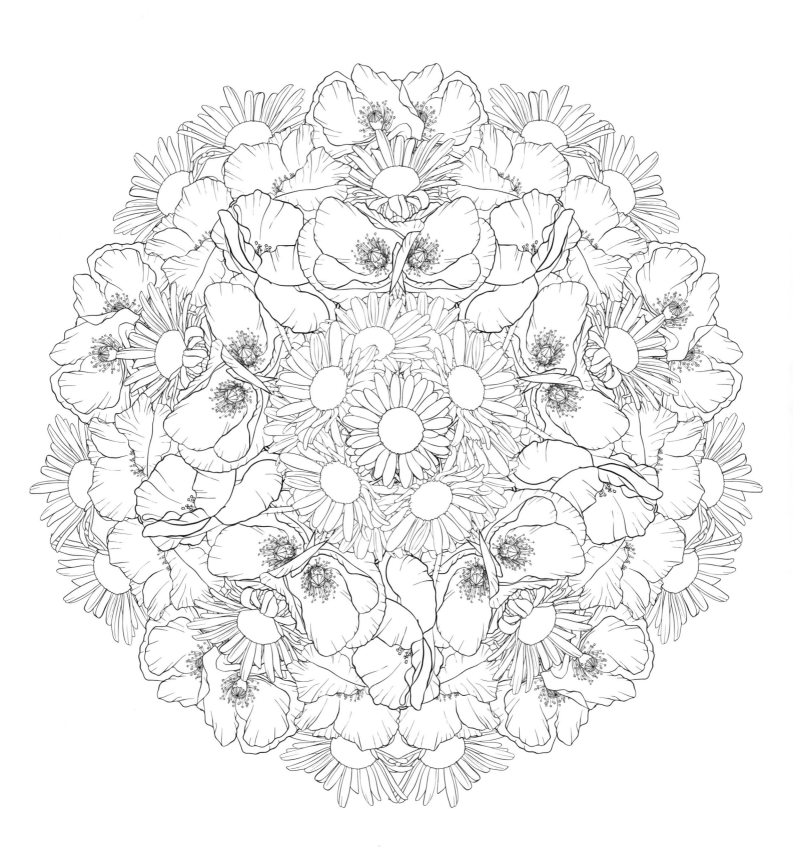